This book belongs to:

Given with love by:

Once upon a time,
in a land far away,
Lived a lovely lady,
whose smile could brighten any day.

Her name was

GRAMMY

AND SHE ADORED A LITTLE ONE,
WHOSE EYES SHONE LIKE DIAMONDS,
AND WHOSE HEART WAS KIND AND FUN.

Grammy

LOVED THOSE BIG BRIGHT EYES,

THEY TWINKLED LIKE THE STARS,

AND IN THEM SHE SAW GREAT BEAUTY

THAT REFLECTED, LIKE JUPITER AND MARS.

WITH THAT LITTLE ONE,

Grammy

SAW SUNSHINE, AND SOMETIMES EVEN RAIN,

BUT MOST OF ALL, SHE SAW THEIR LOVE,

THAT NOTHING COULD RESTRAIN.

THEIRS WAS A LOVE THAT GREW STRONGER,
WITH EACH PASSING DAY,
AND IT WARMED THE WORLD,
LIKE SUNSHINE'S GOLDEN RAY.

With no limit or condition,
their love shone bright and true,
For that

Grammy

knew that love was the
greatest gift she ever knew.

Grammy's

LOVE WAS LIKE A COMPASS
THAT ALWAYS KNEW THE RIGHT WAY,
HER LOVE NEVER GOT LOST,
EVEN ON A WINDY DAY.

They enjoyed talking, and walking,
and sharing some snacks.
while the bright sun
beamed down warmly on their backs.

They would bake cookies,
and find something fun to do.
They would go on wild adventures,
and explore something new.

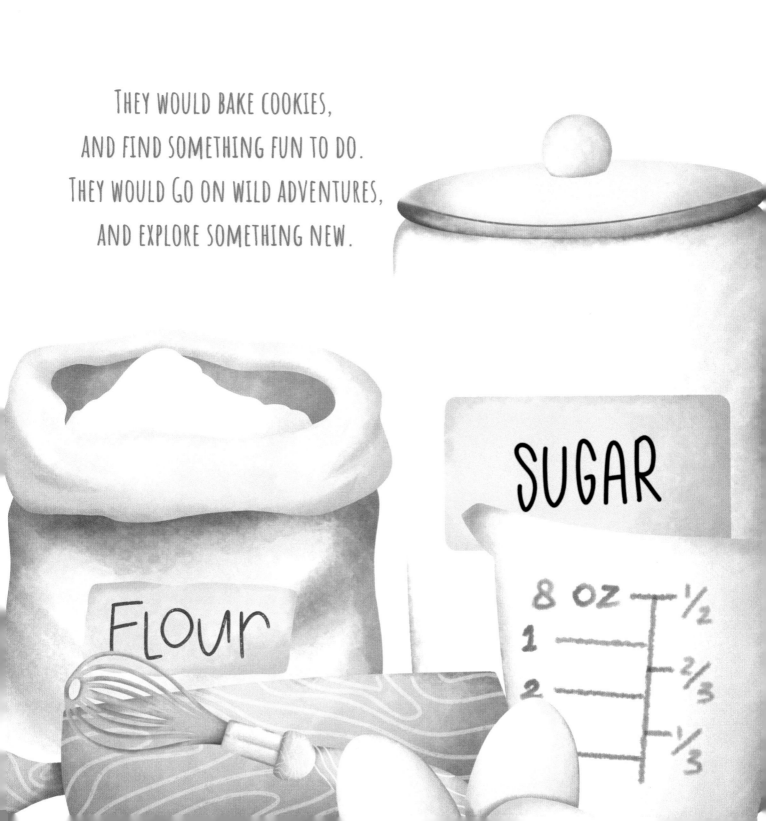

The little one loved when

Grammy

would read stories aloud,
Or when they would have
picnics under a shady cloud.

Grammy's

LOVE WAS BIGGER THAN MOUNTAINS SO GRAND,

IT STRETCHED SO FAR AND WIDE,

ACROSS THE SEA AND LAND.

The memories they shared,
would last a lifetime and more,
And even when they were apart,
their love would still soar.

They always had something to share;
A phone call, a hug, a toy, a treat, or
a special trip to the fair.

Just like this story,
There is someone so dear....
who wants to show you,
that her love is always near!

So please remember,
dear little one,
That you have a
Grammy
Who loves you a ton.

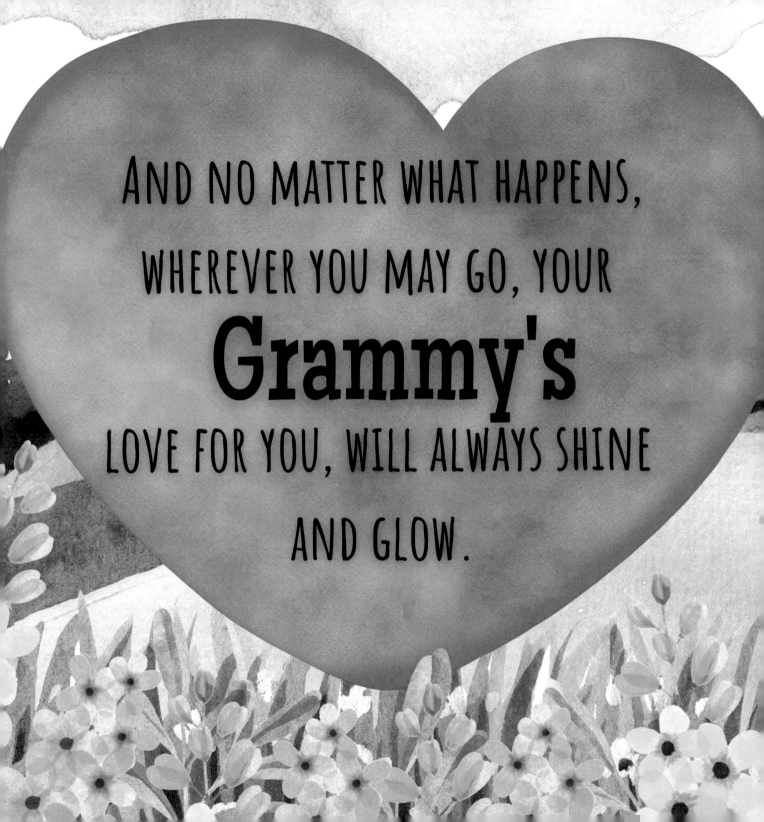

AND NO MATTER WHAT HAPPENS, WHEREVER YOU MAY GO, YOUR **Grammy's** LOVE FOR YOU, WILL ALWAYS SHINE AND GLOW.

Made in United States
Orlando, FL
16 July 2025